CAP

D0646437

J
745.54   Bliss, Helen,
BLI   Paper

CAP 1/2010   LSB 4/2000
reassign 9

SANTA CRUZ PUBLIC LIBRARY
Santa Cruz, California

CAP

Paper

Helen Bliss

Crabtree Publishing Company

SANTA CRUZ PUBLIC LIBRARY
Santa Cruz, California

Craft Workshop

Crabtree Publishing Company

350 Fifth Avenue	360 York Road, R.R.4	73 Lime Walk
Suite 3308	Niagara-on-the-Lake	Headington, Oxford
New York, NY 10118	Ontario L0S 1J0	England OX3 7AD

Edited by **Virginia Mainprize**
Designed by **Jane Warring**
Illustrated by **Lindy Norton**
Photography by **Steve Shott**

Children's work by
**George Abraham, Sarah Berjerano, Daniel Bergsagel,
Ilana Bergsagel, Camilla Bliss-Williams, Raffy Bliss-Williams,
Caroline Bresgers, Florrie Campbell, Livonia Demetriou, Joshua Hay,
Daniel Hilton, Matthew McDougal, Miranda Segal, Amy Williams**

Created by

Thumbprint Books

Copyright © 1998 Thumbprint Books
All rights reserved. No part of this publication may be reproduced in any form
or by any means - graphic, electronic or mechanical, including photocopying,
recording, taping or information storage and retrieval systems -
without prior permission in writing of the publishers.

Cataloging-in-Publication Data

Bliss, Helen, 1955-
Paper / Helen Bliss.
p.   cm. – (Craft Workshop)
Includes index.
Summary: Provides instructions for creating different kinds of paper and a variety of items,
including animals, gift wrap, greeting cards, masks, and more, from these papers.
ISBN 0-86505-791-5 (pbk). – ISBN 0-86505-781-8 (rhb)
1. Paper work– Juvenile literature.[1. Paper work. 2. Handicraft.]
I. Title. II. Series.
TT870.B545 1998   745.54 -- dc21   97-32134

CIP

AC

Printed in Hong Kong by Wing King Tong Co Ltd

First published in 1998 by
A & C Black (Publishers) Limited
35 Bedford Row, London WC1R 4JH

Cover picture: This paper cut shows two roosters sitting on a Tree of Life. Paper cuts like this were
made to decorate Polish houses at Easter time.

Contents

So many uses

Think how different the world would be without paper. There would be no books, comics or newspapers to read. There would be no letters, paper money or photographs.

Before paper was invented, people carved words and messages into stone or clay. Later, people wrote on scraped and dried animals skins, called parchment. Stone, clay and parchment are difficult to write on, heavy and hard to store.

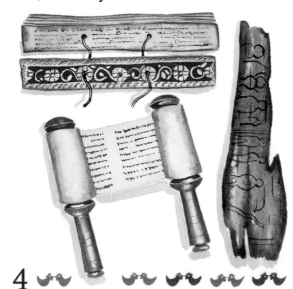

Paper was invented almost 2,000 years ago. Ts'ai Lun, an official at the court of the Chinese emperor, soaked old fish nets, rags and leaves in boiling water. He pounded the mixture until it became a mushy pulp. When the pulp dried, it turned into paper.

Even after paper was invented, books were very expensive because they were all copied by hand. People continued to write on parchment because it was strong and lasted for hundreds of years. When the printing press was invented in 1450, books could be copied cheaply and quickly on paper. Then, people began using paper instead of parchment.

For a long time, paper was made from cotton and linen rags. Today, most paper comes from wood that is crushed into pulp inside huge machines. Millions of trees are planted each year just for making paper. Used paper can be recycled into new paper.

People have learned to color paper with dyes. They decorate it by printing pictures and patterns onto it. People also cut, shape and layer paper to make beautiful and useful things.

Look at the pictures of things other children have made with paper. Use their ideas for your own projects.

You can make great gifts for your family and friends.

This books shows six ways of working with paper. It tells how to make, decorate and cut paper.

Tools and tricks

You will need paper, paints, scissors and glue for the projects in this book.

Paper

For paper cuts, thin, colored paper is best. For fine paper cuts, use tissue paper. You can recycle newspaper or office paper to make pulp for molding and shaping. Use only white paper for handmade paper because the color in printed paper will make 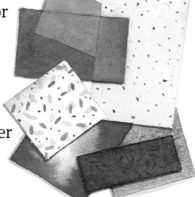 your paper gray. Newspaper and comics are great for layering. For the stretched paper projects, use large sheets of paper.

Scissors

Paper scissors are fine for most projects. For paper cuts you will need small, pointed scissors. Try using pinking shears with zig-zag blades to make your cut-outs different.

Simple snip tricks

To make holes on the inside of your paper cuts, gently pinch the paper between your thumb and forefinger. Snip off the end of the pinched paper. This makes a hole which you can cut bigger.

How to make paper pulp

Fill one-third of a large pail with paper torn into small pieces. Ask an adult to add enough hot water to cover the paper. Let it soak and cool for twenty minutes. Stir it hard with a wooden spoon until the paper begins to turn to mush.

Put about ¼ cup (65 ml) of this mixture into a blender or food processor. Cover the paper with water. Ask an adult to keep turning the machine on and off so as not to strain the motor. Blend the mixture until smooth. Pour the pulp into a container. Repeat until all the paper is blended. It can be kept covered in the refrigerator.

How to mold paper

Put the pulp into a sieve. Drain off as much water as you can. Put the pulp in a bowl and stir in 1 cup (250 ml) of white craft glue. Plastic margarine tubs, foil and styrofoam food containers, plates and bowls can be used as shapes for molding paper. Cover one side of the mold with plastic wrap. Pat on a 1 inch (2.5 cm) layer of paper pulp. Let the pulp dry completely.

How to layer a paper mask

Put a blown-up balloon into a bowl. This will keep the balloon steady while you work. Tear old newspaper into 2 inch (5 cm) pieces. Mix equal amounts of white craft glue and water in a bowl. Dip the newspaper pieces, one by one, into the glue.

Cover the front half of the balloon with the pieces of newspaper. Make sure the pieces overlap one another. Keep adding pieces of newspaper until you have five layers. Let the paper dry.

Making eye holes on a paper mask

Put the mask up to your face. Ask a friend to draw circles on it where your eyes are. Because the paper is very hard, ask an adult to cut out the eye holes with sharp scissors.

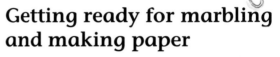

Getting ready for marbling and making paper

Marbling and paper making are wet activities. Cover a table with lots of newspaper to soak up the water. You may also want to spread newspaper on the floor. Wear an old shirt or apron and a pair of rubber gloves.

After marbling, ask an adult to help you clean up with paint thinner. Wash your hands well with soap and water.

Pretty paper cuts

In China, people have been making paper cuts for centuries. They were used as decorations and good luck charms. Today, people all over the world still use paper cuts for decorations at festivals, parties, weddings and even funerals.

Cai Xiaoli

A Chinese artist made a paper cut of this tiger cat to pin on the bed of a newborn child. The paper cut is supposed to protect and amuse the baby. The color red means joy.

The Chinese also make paper cuts to hang on their walls and windows. They use them to decorate their shoes and clothes. All the pictures have special meanings.

In Mexico, these colorful banners are made of tissue paper. On special days, such as Christmas and the Day of the Dead, they are hung across streets and between trees.

Mexican artists make these banners by hand. They stack fifty sheets of tissue paper in a pile. They cut a design through the whole pile with a hammer and a sharp chisel.

In Poland, people cleaned and painted their cottages before Easter. Each year, they made new paper cuts to decorate their homes.

Polish people in Kurpie used sheep shears to cut a Tree of Life from a single sheet of paper. They also made cut-outs, like this bright bird, with different colors of paper.

In the Lowicz region of Poland, people created colorful cut-outs of rows of people. Some are wearing the costumes of the region. Others are dancing, playing music, or traveling by horse or bicycle. The cut-outs were made from pieces of paper glued in a row.

Colorful cut-outs

Make your own paper cuts from colored paper. Try using pinking shears with zig-zag blades for interesting designs. For fine cutting, use small, sharp scissors. Start with simple shapes. Later, you can try more detailed patterns.

The Tree of Life

Fold a large piece of colored paper in half. Draw the outline of one half of a tree on one side, with its trunk on the fold. You can make the branches swirly or straight. You may want to add leaves and birds. Carefully cut around the outline of the tree. Do not cut along the fold. Open up the paper to see your Tree of Life.

Amazing animals

On colored paper, draw the outline of a dragon-dog, bird-fish or other imaginary animal. Draw on shapes and patterns. Cut out your animal. Cut out the inner lines using the snip method. (See page 6 for instructions.)

Make a bird in the same way. Cut out shapes from other pieces of colored paper. Glue some on top of your bird. Glue others under the snipped-out holes.

Festive flags

Make cut-outs to string together into a banner for your room or for a party. Draw bold designs on pieces of tissue paper, but leave a wide border at the top of each piece. Shade in the bits you want to cut out. With thin, sharp scissors, snip out the shaded parts. Put the finished flags in a row. Lay a long piece of string below their top edges. Fold the edges over the string and glue them down.

Decorated paper

The earliest patterned papers were left at Japanese temples as prayer offerings. Since then, hand-decorated paper has been used for books, boxes, picture frames and wallpaper.

These swirls are made by dropping colored inks into gel. A pattern is drawn in the inks with a stick. When a sheet of paper is put on top of the gel, the inks stick to the paper. This way of decorating is called marbling.

In ancient Japan, wonderful patterns were made by blowing the inks into strange shapes. In Turkey, thin needles were used to draw flower shapes in the inks. Brushes and combs are also used to create beautiful patterns.

Solveig Stone, Compton Marbling

Another way of marbling is to drop oil paint onto water and swirl it into patterns. Because oil does not mix with water, the patterns keep their shape. When a sheet of paper is put on top, paint sticks to it.

These boxes are covered with paste paper. It is made by brushing colored flour paste on a sheet of paper.

A comb, stick or a finger is dragged through the paste while it is wet. These patterns show the paper underneath.

People in the mountains of Nepal make paper by boiling bark into a pulpy mush. It is sieved, made into flat sheets, and dried. Artists decorate the paper by printing wood block pictures onto it. They use ink made from plants.

Patterns and prints

Make your own decorated paper for covering books and boxes or wrapping gifts for your family and friends. You can use almost any kind of paper. Try using tissue or brown wrapping paper.

Magic marbling

This is a very messy job, so cover your work area with newspaper and ask an adult to help you. Mix equal amounts of oil paint and paint thinner in a jar. Use a separate jar for each color. You will need only a little of each.

Line a baking pan with layers of aluminum foil. Fill it almost to the top with water. Slowly pour the paints onto the water and swirl them gently with a stick. Do not over mix. Wearing rubber gloves, float a sheet of paper on top of the water, making sure there are no air bubbles. Do not let the paper soak. Lift the paper off the water. Let the extra paint and water drip into the pan. Put the paper, paint side up, onto newspapers to dry.

Printed papers

Draw designs onto thin sponges with a felt-tipped pen. Cut out the pieces with small, sharp scissors. Cut pieces of corrugated cardboard a little larger than the sponge shapes. Glue each shape to a piece of cardboard with waterproof glue.

Dab a sponge shape into some water-based paint. Press the sponge gently onto a sheet of paper. Mix and match shapes and colors to print a pattern all over the paper.

Dragged designs

Mix 2 tablespoons (30 ml) of cornstarch with 1 cup (250 ml) of water in a pot. Ask an adult to stir the mixture on low heat until it is clear. Let it cool. Mix in some paint. Brush the colored paste onto a sheet of paper. Draw patterns with your fingers or a comb.

15

Handmade paper

Paper has been made by hand for almost 2,000 years. In Nepal and Japan, handmade papers are still created by the same methods that papermakers have used for centuries.

Handmade paper is made from a mushy pulp of ground-up rags and hot water. When the pulp dries, the threads tangle together to form a sheet of paper. Banana leaves and sugar cane can also be used to make paper.

The paper shown above is made only once a year in France. In the summer, papermakers collect and press flowers from the meadows. They mix them into the wet pulp so that the flowers become part of the paper as it dries.

To make paper pulp, rags or plants are soaked and pounded into mush in a vat of boiling water. Two frames, called a mold and deckle, are scooped into the vat and lifted out again. Water drains through the wire mesh of the mold, leaving a layer that turns into paper when it dries.

mold

deckle

These papers come from the villages of southern India. They are made from recycled rags and are very strong. Artists print or paint pictures and patterns onto the paper.

Washi, or fine Japanese paper, is made from the bark of the mulberry tree. The pink paper in the picture below was made by mixing cotton threads and shiny golden flecks into pulp. The lacy look was created by dripping water through a stencil onto freshly made paper.

Pulp and paper

Make your own paper using the instructions on page 6. You can dye the pulp any color you like. Decorate it with seeds or flowers. You can make paper pulp pictures. This paper is also great for greeting cards.

Flowery fun

Lay an old dish cloth on top of layers of newspaper. Spread pulp onto the cloth. Lay pressed flowers and leaves onto the pulp. Put another cloth on top. Gently roll it with a rolling pin. Remove the top cloth and let the pulp dry. Try using bits of foil, sequins or wool instead of flowers.

Pasta and seeds

Mix acrylic or powder paint into ½ cup (125 ml) of paper pulp to color it. Stir in some seeds, dried lentils, beans or pasta. Cover your work area with a thick layer of newspaper. Lay an old dish cloth on top.

Spread the pulp evenly over the cloth, shaping it into a rectangle. Lay a second cloth on top. Press it gently all over with your hands or a rolling pin. Peel off the top cloth. Let the pulp dry and become a piece of decorated paper.

Pulpy pictures

Make different colors of pulp using colored paper.

Spread a dish cloth on top of a thick layer of newspaper. Shape a picture on the cloth using the different colors of pulp. You can layer one color on top of the other, or you can put the colors side by side. Put another cloth on top of your picture. Press it gently to squeeze out the water. Take off the top cloth and let your picture dry.

Painted pulp

Paper pulp is cheap and easy to mold.
For centuries, people all over the world
have used it to make useful and beautiful
objects. It is so strong that it can
be made into tables and chairs
and even a soldier's helmet.

This decorated paper
plate comes from Russia.
It is painted in the 'Khokhloma'
style. Four hundred years ago,
Khokhloma was an important fort.
Farmers came there to sell hand-
painted wooden bowls and spoons.

Today, plates like
this are molded from
paper pulp in Russian factories.
Artists paint leaves, bright flowers and
berries on them in red, black and gold.
They paint these right onto the plates
without drawing an outline.

These model animals come from Bihar in northeastern India. Women have been making these paper pulp toys for their children for centuries. About thirty years ago, the crops failed in Bihar. To buy food for their families, people began making these toys to sell to tourists.

These paper pulp boxes come from Kashmir in northern India. They were made first from pulp left over from papermaking. They held camel-hair brushes used for the tiny details in miniature painting. Today in Kashmir, pulp paper is molded into many other things, such as bowls, candlesticks and picture frames.

Mashed magic

You, too, can turn gray paper pulp into fabulous animals, plates and boxes. Look at the instructions for making and molding pulp on pages 6 and 7.

Bunny dish

With plastic wrap, cover the outside of two bowls that are exactly the same size. Spread a layer of pulp about ⅛ - ¼ inch (25-50 mm) thick over the plastic. Shape a bunny out of more pulp. Press it onto one of the wet pulp bowls. Cut out cardboard ears and stick them into the bunny's head.

When the pulp is dry, lift off the pulp bowls. Peel off the plastic wrap. Trim the edges of the bowls so they fit together. Paint your dish with bright colors.

Pulpy plates

Cover the top of a plate with plastic wrap, leaving some to hang over the sides. With your fingers, spread a layer of pulp about ⅛ - ¼ inch (25-50 mm) thick all over the plate. Pat the pulp down to make it as smooth as possible. Let the pulp dry in a warm place.

Lift the pulp plate off the china plate. Peel off the plastic wrap. Paint your plate in bold colors and decorate it with painted flowers and animals. You can varnish it later to make it shiny.

Animal art

Shape pulp into real or imaginary animals. If you want to make an animal with a long neck or long legs, use sticks or twigs to hold up the pulp. Let your animals dry before you paint and varnish them.

Layered paper

Layers of paper can be glued onto a shape. The paper hardens into an exact copy of the mold. For centuries, artists have made puppet faces, figures and masks in this easy and inexpensive way.

Look at the friendly bear and the wicked wolf licking its lips. They are hand puppets of animals from folk stories. Their heads are hollow and are made from layered paper. Puppeteers can make these animals' heads move.

A puppet head is shaped from clay. Layers of paper are glued on top. When the paper head is dry, it is cut in half, and the clay mold is removed. The paper head is stuck together again with more paper layers.

These masks are worn by Japanese actors. They use them in plays at village festivals.

Some masks are of gods and demons. Others are faces of animals, such as a fox or a monkey. Each face has a special expression which the audience can recognize.

In Italy, in the 1700s, small groups of actors traveled from town to town. They performed funny, masked plays, called *commedia dell'arte*.

The same characters appeared in each play. The actors wore layered paper masks to show which character they were playing. Because the masks covered their eyes and nose, the actors had to show changes of mood with their mouth.

Every year, in November, Mexicans celebrate the Day of the Dead, when they remember relatives who have died. Families decorate their house and bring food to the cemetery.

People make wire and paper skeletons as decorations for the Day of the Dead. They are brightly dressed and look as if they are doing everyday things, such as eating or riding a bicycle.

Loads of layers

You can make layered paper masks for dress-up parties. Layered paper is also perfect for puppet heads and models. All you need is a shape on which to layer the paper. A blown-up balloon, crunched-up paper, pipe cleaners or soft wire all can be used to make a shape.

Marvelous masks

Cover one half of a balloon with five layers of newspaper. (See page 7 for instructions.) If you want to add ears and a nose, glue on crunched-up newspaper. Let the newspaper dry completely, then remove the balloon.

Mark two spots for your eyes and cut out holes. (See page 7 for instructions.) Paint and decorate your mask. Make a small hole on each side and tie a piece of string or elastic to each hole. Your mask is ready to wear.

Playful puppets

Crunch up some newspaper into a ball. Push a short cardboard tube into it and tape them together. This will be your puppet's head and neck. Glue five layers of newspaper onto the head and neck. (See page 7 for instructions.) Glue on crunched-up paper ears and a nose.

When the paper is completely dry, paint the face. Cut two identical pieces of felt in the shape of a dress with long sleeves. Sew or glue the edges of the felt together. Make sure the neck of the dress fits around the cardboard neck. Decorate the dress with felt or ribbon. Glue on hands made of paper or felt.

Wiry wonders

Bend soft wire or pipe cleaners into the shape of a hollow animal, bird or person. To make your shape really strong, tape the wires together with masking tape.

Carefully stuff the wire model with crunched-up tissue paper or polyester stuffing. Loosely wind masking tape over the shape to hold the stuffing. Brush white glue over the masking tape. Stick on several layers of tissue paper strips, spreading more glue over each layer. When it is completely dry, paint your model.

Festivals and fun

For centuries, people in China and Japan have made useful objects by stretching paper over wooden frames. Things made in this way are light and strong. The inside walls of Japanese houses were often made of stretched paper.

To celebrate the new year, Chinese people all over the world gather in the street for a big parade. Children wear lion headdresses like this one. They are made of bamboo and paper.

Dancing men carry a long paper lion on sticks. They shake the lion's huge head and twist its body to the beat of drums. Chinese parades are always fun and noisy.

Each spring in China and Japan there are kite festivals. The kites are made of paper and bamboo. They are painted with pictures of animals or ancient warriors. Some kites are so big that dozens of people are needed to control them. People glue powdered glass onto their kite strings. This makes them razor sharp so they can cut through the strings of other kites.

In Japan, before electric lights, people used paper lanterns with candles inside to light their homes.

Small folding paper lanterns were used for traveling.

This toro, or religious lantern, is made from paper and hangs outside a Buddhist temple. Toro lanterns gave light to monks during their long, nighttime meditations. They were also used to light the altar.

Kites of silk and bamboo were flown in China 3,000 years ago. There are wonderful stories of soldiers strapped to kites, floating high in the sky and spying on the enemy. Kites were also used in religious ceremonies. They were seen as a link between earth and heaven.

Stretched shapes

To make a kite, shadow lamp or headdress, use large sheets of thin paper and bamboo garden sticks (for straight shapes) or bendable plastic sticks (for rounded shapes.)

Kite wall decoration

Bend three plastic sticks and tape them together with masking tape, as shown in the picture. Tape these shapes and four straight sticks together to make a frame.

Coat one side of the frame with strong glue. Press the frame onto a big sheet of thin paper. When the glue is dry, trim the paper all around the edges of the frame. Wipe a damp cloth all over the paper, so it will shrink as it dries. Paint on your design with watercolors.

Shadow lamp

Join eight straight sticks into a pyramid shape with wire and masking tape. Cut four triangles of thin paper, ½ inch (1 cm) larger than each side of the pyramid. Attach the paper to the sides with strong glue.

When the glue has dried, trim off the edges of the paper. Cut out some tissue paper shapes, such as flowers, trees, stars or animals. Stick them onto the inside of the lamp with a glue stick. In a dark room, put a flashlight inside your lamp and watch the shadows!

Monster headdress

Wire and tape sticks together to make a strong pyramid frame. It should be large enough for you to put your head inside. You can add extra sticks to make your headdress even bigger.

Cover the frame with thin paper as you would to make a shadow lamp. Leave one section open for your head. Decorate the headdress with bright watercolors, feathers, pieces of wool or ribbon, candy wrappers and sequins.

Index

Acknowledgements

The publishers are grateful to the following for permission to reproduce the illustrations on the pages mentioned.
Page 8: Cai Xiaoli; page 13: Solveig Stone, Compton Marbling; page 28: Ray Man Musical Instruments.

1 2 3 4 5 6 7 8 9 0 Printed in Hong Kong 7 6 5 4 3 2 1 0 9 8

0000112715701